DEATH

SONG

DEATH
SONG

Thomas McGrath

EDITED BY SAM HAMILL

INTRODUCTION BY

DALE JACOBSON

COPPER CANYON PRESS / PORT TOWNSEND

Some of the poems in this book have appeared in the following publications:

Aluminum Canoe, American Poetry Review, Best Minds Anthology,
Everywhere, Milkweed Chronicle, New Letters, North Dakota Quarterly, Paper
Air, Poetry East, Redstart, Singing Horse, Subversive Agent, The Spirit That
Moves Us, Three Seasons, TriQuarterly, and *Willow Springs.*

The editor wishes to acknowledge his sincere gratitude to Abigail Potvin Jensen,
who served as Thomas McGrath's assistant during the last year of his life,
copying poems, reading and writing letters, compiling manuscripts, and
handling all manner of detail with alacrity.

The publication of this book was supported by a grant from the
National Endowment for the Arts.

Copper Canyon Press is in residence with Centrum at Fort Worden State Park.

COPPER CANYON PRESS
Post Office Box 271
Port Townsend, Washington 98368

TO MY SON
TOM

CONTENTS

I

I I

I I I

I V

INTRODUCTION

"You have enlarged us all and lightened our steps on the mountain." With this line, in his tribute to Rubén Darío (page 31), McGrath provides us with one of the purposes of poetry: its communal affirmation which saves us from diminishing beneath the weight of solitary despair. Poetry carries the capacity to magnify ourselves by giving us each other, transforming our isolation into potential communal nurturing, even celebration. It transforms the oppressive work of being alone into mutual encouragement and vibrancy. For a poet whose range is so enormous, it could well be a presumption to suggest a leitmotif – and yet, the deliverance of the individual from the stasis of isolation is one of McGrath's recurring messages. Not only do his poems show us the need to be nourished by the emotional exchange of community, but they also reveal the depth of that need: community is a necessity that goes to the core of our own sense of value. Our identity can be properly experienced only through and with others.

In his exploration of our communal necessities, we see in McGrath's work the consequences of being removed from the saving (and freeing) connection to people. These consequences are the degenerate effects of isolation, which create a solipsistic world where eventually the individual, rather than discovering and enhancing oneself, becomes lost in a terrifying monotony, a near fatal ennui. This is not the solitude that nurtures by allowing the individual to assimilate and rejuvenate the social world within oneself, but it is a deadening of the world in general that leads to a kind of ubiquitous emptiness in which everything becomes the same. In the poem "Suspicion of Some Kinds of Solitude" (page 16), he writes:

Been here too long.
These roads where only dead men have walked
Open...
Indeed open...

The solitude invents us:
And into our empty souls flies everything that is loose.

Here, instead of discovering our identity, we lose it. The world remakes us in its image, according to its random, haphazard whims. It has the effect of devouring us – all values become equal.

On the other hand, in a poem where we might expect solitude we encounter a kind of second kinship, which is consoling against the harsh and inhospitable indifference of winter:

COLD WINTER NIGHT

We cannot see them
But even behind the mountain
The moon has friends.

(page 53)

Through our shared social enterprise and our personal translation of those feelings, we can *imagine* how others whom we do not know might also admire this same moon. Part of the mystery of this poem is our not knowing who – or what – these friends are, and yet, the experience of friendship, through the common moon, with these unseen others makes the world more familiar.

Poems in this book express our sense of belonging to the universe, the deep sense of its mystery which is also ours. These poems bring us near to the primordial source where we experience a feeling of oneness with all things despite the oppositions on which the universe is built:

SOME THINGS ARE KNOWN

Evening.
The swallows
Like shadows in the far meadow

Diving
    diving. . .

Secret water!
    (page 48)

While this poem provides us with the sense of affinity with the swallows by awakening us to our own mystery through theirs, it still regards them as separate in their own world. Nature is never "expropriated" by McGrath as a device to mirror ourselves – it keeps its wildness. He doesn't diminish its differences, or ours. Still, the sense of community is never lost in his work, nor is it limited to human beings, but he extends it to nature as easily as to ourselves, though unlike Robinson Jeffers, McGrath is not romantic in his connection to nature. We do not see him exalt nature over people or society, nor does he desire to return to the unconscious life of nature. Rather, he cherishes it. We find all sorts of wild birds, animals and insects in these poems. While on one level the poems express nature's dialectical laws that require change by which everything must depart, there is also a strong tenderness and appreciation for the company, the presence, of this various life of nature:

WINTER GOODNIGHT

The first deep frost
Of a cold autumn
Beautiful! On the flowers and grass.

But I miss the last song
Of my frozen cricket. . .
    (page 54)

The poem "Slaughterhouse Music," (page 13) is presented in the voice of the cattle arriving from the train cars to the stockyard pens. Here community is not expressed in terms of the poet's feeling toward the animals, but in terms of the animals' feelings to-

ward each other. Initially, the cattle send their "separate cries /
Into the open range beyond the wire [. . .] Barbaric discords."
However, as the cattle come closer to the realization of their im-
pending deaths, their voices become more and more a communal
choir of solidarity, "Despair and defiance / To shout down all the
pens." Again, we see that community is not a feeling limited to
human beings. The suggestion implicit in McGrath's view of com-
munity is that it is not our invention, but rather, it is an inherent
need deeply rooted within us. Thus, if in our social situation,
communal feeling is unattainable, we become alienated not only
from society, but also from ourselves.

For McGrath, the highest quality of community is solidarity.
Human solidarity, however, does not remain only an unconscious
emotional need, but it becomes also a reality of consciousness. If
extended to the historical process of capitalism, under which the
fierce production of capital all but denies the workers who produce
it, solidarity takes on a political significance. McGrath's poetry
expands solidarity beyond our private lives into the political
world. One example of this is in the poem "There Is Also A
Fourth Body" (page 32), written in response to the poem by
Robert Bly, "A Man and a Woman Sit Near Each Other." In Bly's
poem, the shared but private world of the man and the woman is
described as "a third body" which they have promised to love. In
McGrath's poem, this shared world, which he calls solidarity, is
"enlarged" (to use his word from his poem to Rubén Darío) so
that it includes not only the feelings that the man and the woman
share between themselves, but also their love for their family and
friends. Part of McGrath's poem reads:

> In the predawn light they are aware of another being:
> Who is themselves and not their own selves: an emanation
> Or ghostsmoke that arises from the sweat of their work and
>   their sex —
> Rises on their breath and the breath of their children
> As their hopes and dreams and those of friends and comrades:
> A longing

a desire

a pledge:

a third body: of Solidarity.

This passage alone puts the third body into a larger connection with the world, but he then goes on to talk of the fourth body, "the spirit of capitalism and exploitation"... "death squads in every barrio of the poor" against which the woman and the man "must raise their little flag. And the barricades of their bodies." As the poem ends, the third body has become a social front, a necessary political solidarity.

Community in McGrath's poetry goes to the core of our existence — and in political terms, as solidarity, it is the one absolutely necessary weapon that can preserve our existence against impoverishment, homelessness, and hunger, while at the same time holding the potential for our freedom. Solidarity is a matter both of survival and identity.

The title of this book alludes to the practice in many American Indian cultures of singing one's own death song. Of particular relevance to the title are the short poems that focus on nature. These poems express the immutable insistence of the dialectical laws for change. There is sometimes a sadness in them, as in the poem "Memory":

> The wild cries
> Fall through the autumn moonlight...
>
> But the geese
> Have already gone.
> (page 49)

At other times there is a mystery, as in the poem "Riddle":

> Dawn light...
> In the cold brook —
> Is it the sky falling?

Or a trout leaping...
Snapping at a star?
             (page 47)

Many of these shorter poems, such as "Riddle," are among the last McGrath wrote. It is danger, loss, and mystery that these poems explore—they put us in the vicinity of the unknown. Nature does not necessarily provide solace or secret comfort—but it is *wild* and unpredictable. No assumptions can be made. As he says in "Poem":

I hear a heavy knocking
In the midnight river.
Something I've never known
Is coming home.
             (page 71)

McGrath doesn't romanticize nature, or idealize the working class. There is no attempt to make nature "spiritual" as a mirror of the individual "soul" or as a place of refuge from society. Nor does he portray the working class as being necessarily in touch with its own interests or needs, as we can see in the poem "A Momentary Loss of Belief in the Wisdom of the Common People and a Curse on the Bastards Who Own and Operate Them" (page 94). Still, his poetry provides us an affirmation against the intense isolation and alienation of our time. It tells us that we are not meant to be alone, that we don't need to accept isolation, and that the world does not exist in a paralyzing stasis. It insists we recognize our humanity in common. In this way, it not only nourishes us, but also enlarges us all.

DALE JACOBSON

6

FOR MY BOOK

Fly up little one
Against the wind!
who wants an easy ride?

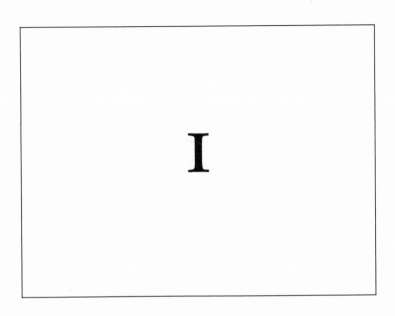

I

THE CRIPPLED ARTIST

1.

Harsh, even to the callous ear,
He scuffs along the street in his coarse boots.
The dreaming citizens, hustling, do not hear –
Or so he thinks. And thinks them blind as bats
Were once thought blind. Propelled into the day
By racking rents, child, wife and holy car
That steers them constant toward a falling star –
Mechanized Christs up on the sacred ways –
And old coots, down cats, whores and tear-aways – they ramble
        all around.

2.

All around him. He thinks he must be glass,
Cloudy, perhaps: smudged, smoky – a bit crazed
Somewhere at center. And so he comes to pass –
Being occulted – to where the rose is prized
By middleclass flowerwallahs gilding the gilded stalk
Of the golden lily in fence protected yards.
Above him fly the bright incontinent birds –
Milwaukee Avenue: his daily walk,
Where now the lengthening autumnal sun gives back the lacquered
        oak leaves' luster.

3.

He'd like to take them home: the flowers, the light –
But all light falters in the narrow room
He paints in – which he wants to call his home.
Half-bat-blind, what does he want? He wants insight

Or outsight: his room blazes like a noon sun-ranch.
When people lose the vision, they think lost.
He does. His paint-hand, like a willow branch,
Twitches, storm-tossed. First things become last.
Still he persists, prizing the fallen light, expendable, now dying
        in the street

4.

And still he struggles: to take them back alive –
Flowers, birds, street, people the light that lies
Still in some alleys. It is a kind of love,
Perhaps, that sends him into those dark ways
To search the wreckage for some living thing:
To celebrate! Breath held, he lifts his arm...
Strength flows to hand...it flies...as if a wing!
And light illuminates all that he loves to praise!
The centuries fall asleep: the adamantine walls soften – scary –

Working, he thinks:
The lyf so short, the craft so long to lere...
Despair so easy. Hope so hard to bear.

SLAUGHTERHOUSE MUSIC

1.

First, we feel the train
Slowing.
Then we see the pens as the train stops.
The doors open.
We leave the excrement-covered floors
Of the cattle cars and the stench of our journey.

A joy to stand in the ankle-deep dust and dried dung of the yards!
Sun?
    And a high blue sky!
We blink in the glare of light and our cries go up:
Bellowings, snorts, grunts, whines, farts and whinnys–
A bedlam of many languages lifts toward heaven.
Then we stampede to the watering troughs and the sparse food.

As evening grows out of the earth,
Uneasy in the failing light
We push at the fences . . .
Moaning and bleating,
Sending our separate cries
Into the openrange beyond the wire . . .
A kind of singing in all our languages
Out . . .
Into the desolation –
The emptiness that we once thought was home.

A kind of singing . . .
Barbaric discords before we lie down to sleep
In the feathery dust and dung.

2.

Morning comes in with the first train.
Others arrive and our lives are repeated.
But the afternoon brings rain
And a new thing:
A ramp at the end of our pen, leading
Up to what we had never noticed:
A vast black iron door.

They want us to ascend: to rise,
To fly up the ramp toward the black iron.
So we are lead, bullied, cajoled, prodded, bulldozed
And we resume our ascensions until – suddenly –
Turning in complaining concert, we look back
And lifting our eyes to the hills – we see:
Everywhere – ! mountain, valley, seacoast, and plain:
Wooden dog-legs, cactus-hedges, thorn-and-wattle, and barbed-wire
        fences:
Pens!
Everywhere!
The whole world a pen. . .
What we had thought unique. . . universal.

3.

The black gate opens on its shuddering hinge.
Our first contingent is cut out and enters.
The door swings. . .
But not before we hear a dull thudding
As of mauls
On wood stumps muffled by animal skins. . .
And we see the flash of axes, rising and falling,
Like puny lightning in the heavy gloom. . .
The door swings shut before we might race in and stop it –

If we could or if we would.
But we still hear and see – as if in dream.
And so we begin to sing.

Not as complaint – but loud!
Despair and defiance
To shout down all the pens and all the stars!
And it seems proper
To sing in solidarity a little while still together –
Before we go under the axe.

SUSPICION OF SOME KINDS OF SOLITUDE

I.

I have been a long time in this emptiness
Most of it wasted...
Out here it is so easy for the fool,
Mad in his isolation,
To mistake the solitude of his own poor soul for a diamond.

These zircons are everywhere!
If you want a really rare diamond
Look for it in a crowd!

I I

Enough! Been here too often!
Friend, do you know how hot are the horns of the deer?
Or in which tree the owl
Has stored his winter silence?

Been here too long.
These roads where only dead men have walked
Open...
Indeed open...

Then solitude invents us:
And into our empty souls flies everything that is loose.

I I I

The solitary man becomes dangerous:
He pumps his soul into everything:
Pump—a frog
Pump—a hawk
Pump—pump—a horse singing in a lost well.

IV

Oh it's too little!
Those useless silences!
Those hawks made only for art!
Those roads leading to Nowhere!

V

North or South...
It's all the same
In the solitudes
Of each other.

TRANSFORMATIONS OF OLD SILVER
CROSSING THE CONTINENT

1.

Sweetly the spoons lie bent in sleep
Deep in their maiden keep
Shaping themselves to their other selves
Spooning and bundling
Cold comforts cold
Dreaming of honey near Omaha
Fearing
      Indians
            black cook pots the. . .
Western Passage.

2.

The forks fire
Through the wooden spokes of the wagon wheels
The forks stand like steel
Then wheel heel to heel
And stand once more like steel
Behind one another
The forks fire and fall back fire and fall. . .
And fall back and fire.
Each fork has two pairs
Of silver tears
Three for himself and one he shares
Into his fellows' fires
To melt down to silver rounds
Where he stands
            fires
              falls.
The Indians do not fear
The forks. They do not care.

They come on
They come on and on
As each fork fires his tear fires and falls.
The forks would like to plant a foot at each
Of the four fell corners of the world of flesh –
They are pioneers with their tears and fears
But the Indians come on
They have no cures or cares for the tears and fears of pioneers.
Their fresh ponies are hurled
Against that silver world
The Indians come
They come on they come on.

3.

The knives, hard featured, do not care.
What had they to share
In the hand-to-mouth finicking
Of forks and spoons?
Their job was to cut the meat.
They did not share the eating.
Such hunger honed an edge . . .
Now, flashing long and spare,
They feel this is not their war.
They are tired of playing the rich man's high-plumed whore
Or pimping for the nice folks and forks and simpering layabout
        spoons.

The Indians come on
Come on and on and on
The knives, sharp-eyed, see but do not fear or care.

They try to tear
The aristocratic crests
From their emblazoned breasts
They sharpen themselves
On their comrades' hardening strength

Honing an insurgent edge
Feeding their appalling blades
Learning to temper the heart
To common desires and all
Our unstayed common need.

The Indians come on
Till bored with forks and spoons they turn and tear away
Tuning arrow and bow
On the trail of the buffalo.

The knives stand quite apart
They do not fall back or start
At sudden peril. They stand,
A palisade of sharpened bayonets
Holding our common ground as staunch
As a band of Indians or outlawed Communists,
Guerrillas, armed, in mountains or jungle mists,
Against all masters all imperialists.

EVEN SONG

Sundown in the Western Lands!

On Ninth Street South in Minnepimp,
(The nihilipolitan double parochial Capitol
Of the Strategic Province of central American emptiness
One of the several United States of the many Americas.)

This village (pronounced UGH) that lies between
The hamlets of *Y'KNOW*...and *WHO:ME?*
On a once-great river...(sweet Afton flow gently)
On Ninth Street South I sit overlooking the slaveway,
Highway 94, and into the wide
Penthouse of the city...
               Burning...
                           in the fallen light...

Below, the cars, bound to their lanes, rush east, rush west
Interchangeable: powered by the mainstream mysteries
Of money, hydrocarbons and high anxiety...

   Take this hammer, HUH!
   Take it to the Captain, HUH!
   Tell him I'm gone, boy...
   Tell him I'm gone

Twilight of lutefisk on the Cloaca-Maxima!

   Don't knock it, Mac,
   Three hundred miles from where you were born?
   You didn't get far either.

THE PLEASURES OF
THE GREAT SALT LAKE

The great salt moon, that plunges at
The sky, and mirror-like reclaims
A Utah of astonishment
And sunlight, snares no second glance
From jaded tourists roaring down
Nevada's tired and faded hills.

The road slants ruler straight; and salt
The world hangs from the tourist eye
Across the salt-crust mesas swim,
Like dinosaurs the shallow sea,
Miraged, or leap and come to rest
Their bases planted on the clouds.

Yet all this fine and ponderous play
Where the Rockies skip like young rams
Does not amuse the voyaging soul.
In mad and dedicated calm,
He eyes the inscape's decorous hills
Or guidebooks' foolproof scenery.

Tired from their weighty levitation
Mountain and mesa settle down
To race at ninety miles an hour
Past the tourist's crawling car,
All their hop-scotch reality
Boring the dull sight-seer's eye.

TRAIL BLAZERS

–remembering Stephen Vincent Benét

Through the Cumberland Gap
To the Wilderness Trace
To the Natchez Trace
Of Stephen Vincent Benét

To Sault Ste. Marie
And Michilimackinac
To Warrior's Path
And to Santa Fe

By the Erie Canal
And the Soo Canal
And the Welland Canal
Up to Montreal

And by the Old Post Road
Up Boston way
Down to Monterey
On El Camino Real

On the Red River Trail
(Either South or North)
To Fargo and Winnipeg
Or toward Fort Worth

On the Bath Bay Express
Toward Union Square
Or to Scollay Square
Or to Rittenhouse Square

Through Dead Man's Pass
In the whirling snow

Toward Happy Camp or Sutter's Mill—
And on we go

On the Bozeman Trail
And the Chisholm Trail
And the Bonner Pass
To Half Moon Bay

On the U.P. the S.P. the cold N.P.
The Salty Dog and the old Katy
Turn right at Texas
Toward Poker Flat
And we'll sleep tonight
In Medicine Hat.

AT PORT TOWNSEND

– for Sam and Tree

1.

O Sea!
All day I've listened to you
Spelling out your monotonous secrets.
We can't *both* fit in this confessional.
One of us has got to go!

2.

So much salt there...
This water has sweated in the sun
More than a working day.

3.

Blue engines of the sound –
Dead silent today – the fires have gone out.
Still, the air stiffens
With marine salt.

4.

How bright they are!
The darkening hours
Of the melancholy bay...

5.

All this dead wood
Just above the tideline –
The sea is preparing coffins...
Today I will not take the ferry!

THE BRAVEST BOAT

I first encounter you as a carragh in the Irish sea
(Myself at my old project: how to swim round the world without
      getting wet).
But when I board you, you turn into a canoe –

And immediately we are shooting the rapids on the last wilderness
      river in the entire world!
And just as I'm getting the hang of it – the patois – you are
      screaming at the run of white water – and

Ahoy! We've turned into a Yankee Clipper, all sails set: main
      gallant, to'gallant, jibs, spinnakers and god knows what –
(We are carrying a cargo of wheat from or to Melbourne
And it's all afire in the holds, the decks are so hot
We have to lie on both our backs at once to keep our bellies from
      burning) when –

Steam is invented and we shoot down the Mississippi –
(*Damn the torpedoes* Farragut said when he saw us).
Beyond New Orleans, as we pick up speed,
Suddenly we're up on the step, and aquaplaning on each other!

     *   *   *

We fly beyond the Mexique Bay to Ensenada!

FOR BORIS GREENFIELD

How far, traveller, have you come from those woolen seasons
In the untranslatable village, where melamed winter
Rapped your knuckles with its stick of cold!
                                        How far
From the Moon of Black Bread, from the Month of Cucumbers,
From the first radish, like a hidden mine
The green tang of its secret ore like a distillation –
Spiritual whiskey – the pure taste of the Spring.
How far you have come, friend, to this Chelm-by-the-Sea,
To the chromium suburbs that can't even pronounce your name!
Country dry as a gourd, where among synthetic gypsies
You meet the second half-century on all fours like a man
Fighting a wild bear. . . .
                                        How strange it must seem
So far from the village and the studious boy,
Here, among friends, where even your children
Must often seem unfamiliar with their outlandish notions. . .
It must have been a hard trek, old friend, I am glad
You have arrived among us.
                                        We, too, are travellers,
Companions of the voyage on the inescapable journey.

FOR LYLA

— Ada, Minnesota, Oct. '85

Champagne for breakfast and bells on all the horses!
Ada rides by, sounding the view halloo!
In pursuit of a matched set of centuries:
Each a brief time-period in which something is seriously wrong.

But to hell with history, I say, entering your house
With its fragrant and resonating clangor of cultures
In which everything denies and sustains its opposite
And the dim dumb denying Lutheran spirit – held at bay.

Forgive my jokes about Uff-Da, Ish-Ta and Who-Da
Whom I once proclaimed the goddesses of Thither Minnesota.
You, Lady, have dispelled their evil charms. For you
The flowers glow at your feet and the fruit falls into your hands.

And forgive my jokes of waking from dreams of exotic bordellos:
The Red Room is now, sedately, the "downstairs study."
Though I still wake to stares of alarmed or alarming ladies
And shelves of their books may collapse on my poor unbloomsburied
        head –

Still I sleep happily, peacefully – stuffed like a Christmas Goose.
After fine food and talk in which we remake the world.
The house walks in its sleep into Arkadee.
And I lie, serene for this night, in the peace of sheltered sleep.

ENVOI

Lady of largesse, lady of bounty
Free and oppressed in Norman County!

28

Lyla's Tao is the Secret Path
For wet-back Mex and County Mounty,
For lame and late and Johnny-Come-Fervent –
Including, pray, yr humble servt
The dim and limping Tom McGrath

A VISIT TO THE HOUSE OF THE POET

—Nicaragua, 1987
Homage to Ruben Daŕio on his birthday

1.

Era un aire suave: the calm and gentle air
Of early morning in little Ciudad Daŕio—
Which opens the eyes of cocks, roosters (even burros)
In a general serenade to the light now opening the leaves

And the brilliant feathery fans of the Nicaraguan trees:
To carry this grand opera of the morning south: down:
The horny and plumed back of the vast flinty cordillera:
Green backbone of the continent under which Quetzalcoatl sleeps.

This arrogant and militant dawn ignites the fuses of sweet...
Flowers: so the whole world seems blazing in subversive colors:
And around the Poet's house the villagers rehearse your natal day.
But I don't believe La Marquesa Eulalie is on this ground:

Though Verlaine may be: lost: in the streets: with the gathering
    crowd.

2.

In the house of the Poet the floor is of polished earth:
Glossed by many bare feet. And here the Nicaraguan soil
Entered him: from below: and was never wholly lost—
Though his boots polished the polished pavements of the polished
    cities of the world.

Two beds: one of wood and rope: hard: where he dreamed: cold:
Of Roosevelt (Teddy) "hunter...invader of our native America."

And a hammock: Marquesa Eulalie: a Parnassian bed:
Verlaine...Banville (!)...dreams made for warm Parisian sleep...

In the northwest corner a stone and earthen stove: where beans
And rice were cooked: as on the brightening street outside:
Now: they cook their beans and rice in front of your tiny
Magnificent house, Poet: in this most powerful place in America:

Where on the beaten, loved, Nicaraguan earth
In *your* yard the children of illiterates now read your poems.

3.

What does fame mean?
                    El Pajaro azul?
                                        Maybe—
Or maybe not. Fame is food for the novitiate poet:
Without it, though stuffed he starves: it staves off bodily hunger,
And is his soul's caviar, his Host, his spiritual whiskey.

The blue bird does not fill the campesina's wish-pot,
Nor does *les sanglots longues des violins* assuage.
Though Verlaine sang lots of songs, the vile winds at auctions
(Sheriffs' sales) blew peasants' lands into El Jefe's banks.

But your fame belongs to all of us now. No one is thankless—
Though it puts no tiles on roof or patio nor thickens the casings
Of cast-off tires from which crafty artisans fashion our sandals.
You have enlarged us all and lightened our steps on the mountain.

And so, as the lamps come on at the end of your day,
You are part of the light in which the village is haloed:
Here: *el palacio del sol* where once you lived and labored.

THERE IS ALSO A FOURTH BODY

—For the Nicaraguan Compañeros

A man and a woman are lying together in the weak but growing light:
In a *jacal*,
      or a hut of bark,
            or of leaves,
                  or under a bridge somewhere
In Nicaragua
      or El Salvador
             Guatemala
                  Mexico or
The U. S. of A. and Everywhere.
                  They are all the same.
                        All different.

In the predawn light they are aware of another being:
Who is themselves and not their own selves: an emanation
Or ghostsmoke that arises from the sweat of their work and their sex—
Rises on their breath and the breath of their children
As their hopes and dreams and those of friends and comrades:
A longing
      a desire
            a pledge:
                the third body: of Solidarity.

And they have come to know that there is also a fourth body:
Decaying but strong: decaying in the husk of the corn
                      making
The coffee bitter
        poisoning their children—
                  an evil being
With a distant accent coca cola and cowboy boots—

The spirit of capitalism and exploitation – a vile spirit
That poisons their wells with the dead bodies of peasants,
That sours the sweat of workers and fills their shoes with stones
That stuffs their beds with barbwire: mortgages: debts –

Plagues of lawyers follow this foul creation as flies Beelzebub:
Rats in the tenements and cops on all the streets:
Death squads in every barrio of the poor:
Disgusting creatures on the benches of all courts: reactionaries and
        racists.

The fourth body spreads its plague on all continents.
But it is out of these pestilential vapors the woman and the man,
Weaving the breaths of the children and their own needs,
Must raise their little flag. And the barricades of their bodies.

The light grows. The night of the poor is ending. Their day
Begins. The day of the poor. But their dream still continues:
The guerrilla alive in the mountains and guns on every tree...
And, in the tumult of markets, coarse but honest bread.

Demon deer with horns of lightning and human bodies
Prance: in late darkness in another part of the forest.
The dreamers need all helpers magical animal human...
Now they wake from enchanted sleep to their murderous day.

GUERRILLAS

– for Don Gordon

"A little farther," the center begs. "Farther!"
"Just a little bit more," plead the cadres and commissars.
"More!" say the comrades who carry the guns in the mountains.
"More! Fucking more!" the peasants in the villages scream.

"The guerrilla is born alive at the edge of the weather,"
Saith the great poet – Gordon, the holy Don.

And they do go on:
From defeat unto defeat.
From defeat and defeat to victory-and-defeat.
From victory-and-defeat to defeat-and-victory.
From defeat-and-victory to victory-and-victory
To victory, victory, victory to final victory –
Carrying the dust of the provinces into the distant cities...

Now the accent at home in the village is heard in the Capitol Square.
And the bread of the rich is given a new definition and taste.

THE COMMUNIST POET IN HELL

Just like Fargo and Harvard!
Daily instruction in politics
By tiny petty
Bourgeois critics and poets—
The ones who voted for Kennedy
Even when he wasn't running.

IN THE MUSEUM AT FORT RANSOM NORTH DAKOTA

The polished remains
Of the breaking plow
That turned the first prairie furrow.
Under glass.

And:
Extinct wild flowers
Buffalo bones
War bonnets
Ancient rusty
Six-shooters.

LEGENDS, HEROES, MYTH-FIGURES AND OTHER AMERICAN LIARS

Start with Davy Crockett –
A legend for hire –
His nose as long
As a telephone wire.

And he fought a b'ar
With his pants on f'ar
And won at the Alamo –
Or someone's a l'ar.

Or take Solomon Snap,
The peddin' man –
Sold a sheep in wolf's clothing
And a bird-out-of-hand –
(And the bush it wasn't in)

And a false false tooth
Made of a mumbly peg
And a squirrel to nest in
Your basic wooden leg;

Or wooden nutmegs
Or the wild north wind:
By the thirty inch yard
Or in powder kegs –

Last seen heading out
To the Western Lands
With a trainload of postholes
For the farmers in Kansas.

Old stormalong began it –
Windjammer from the sea –

Who made windies and lies
Part of our history

Or maybe Barney Beal
Who could knock down a bull
Until the bull got so deep
He went over the hill.

Or Sam Patch the mill-
Hand – made clothes without seams:
Stripped away our fig leaves
And clothed us in jeans

Or in moon-milky habiliments –
A patch on our pride –
Or in spangled chaparejos
In which to ride

Westward, always westerly,
Toward all desires,
Toward mountain and ocean
And the great Western liars:

Mike Fink, Joe Stink –
Who gave the lie luster –
Helped by Windy Bill
And G. A. Custer.

So the nation became

What legend made of it:

Half exaggeration

Half pure bullshit.

HOW THE REVOLUTION WAS BETRAYED

For Att. Benjy Muggles
a "friend of the People"

Hey, Mr. Anarchloosis Fink!
I saw you and eff bee eye wink.
What are the militants to think,
You wobberly slobberly Cokey gink?
Every poor sod you ever defended —
Six feet under law or deep in the clink.
You meatheaded blackstoned son-of-a-bitch —
Hey, Mr. Anarchloosis Fink!
You stink, you stink, you stink, you stink!

A FABLE FOR POETS

Once upon a time in North Dakota, there was a tribe known as the Harum Scarum Indians. They were great singers and great horse traders and so they had fabulous song cycles and great herds of beautiful horses. One night, after everybody had sung him her or itself to sleep, and even the crickets were silent, the Crows came over the horizon and ran off the whole horse herd.

This caused a commotion in the Harum Scarum village and everyone went charging out in the moonlight only to see their horses disappearing across the great northern plains. Then they started calling their horses and singing to their horses and cajoling them and conjuring them and doing everything possible to bring them back. Half of the horses came back. The vocabulary of half the tribe went West with the Crows, who didn't want it.

The horses that came back and went to the people who had lost all their songs and all their curses, had no words, but the horses came to them. On the other hand, the ones who kept their language, their stories, their curses and their great songs, didn't get *any* horses and were stricken by a mysterious partial paralysis.

This led the Harum Scarum to a proverb:

> The singers cannot ride;
> The riders have no songs.

II

VISIONS...JOURNEYS...

The way in
And the way out
Are the same.

Yes.
And the way to,
And the way from,
Are the same.

But not
If we are going
Somewhere.

MORE NEWS FROM THE LABYRINTH

No.
The way in
And the way out:
Not the same...

But how can we tell?

ANOTHER QUANDARY

I tell myself each day:
Joy lies beyond despair.
But how can I get there
When I stand in my own way?

BAD CESS

I wrote to warn the bourgeoisie once:
"I just want you to know you can *not* count on me!"
Ever since then,
My friends regard me with suspicion.

THAN NEVER

When you wake anywhere to gunfire and revolution
You'll know you're there.
Late!
But not *too* late.

A FATALITY

Here is the deadly old iron bridge.

Somewhere a child is being born.

It will be exactly here.
Sometime...then.

COLD CEREMONY

"Stack the corn here,"
My father says,

November.
We slowly build
The crumbling altar.

PIECES OF STRING

Pick up the last
Fallen apple.
The frost
            has charred it. . .
But what sweetness
Remains
Must last the winter.

RIDDLE

Dawn light. . .
In the cold brook –
Is it the sky falling?

Or a trout leaping. . .
Snapping at a star?

SOME THINGS ARE KNOWN

Evening.
The swallows
Like shadows in the far meadow
Diving
       diving. . .

Secret water!

THE OWL

A stone falls into the moon of the pond
At the center of his rings of sound.

ALWAYS AHEAD OF OURSELVES

September: all bloom and blaze.
Out on the calm and satisfied blue,
Where the lake water ends in the sky,
The geese
Argue
About leaving the country.

MEMORY

The wild cries
Fall through the autumn moonlight...

But the geese
Have already gone.

INAPPROPRIATE LONGING

All winter the lake water,
Under its rafters of ice,
Wonders:
What has happened
To the gulls?

HO HO, THE CARRION CROW

At first light
The earliest crows
Come by:
Still looking for any
Left-over darkness...

SANCTUARY

Swallows nesting under the barn roofs
And pheasants eating among the hens . . .

Must be a poor man's farm –
People too busy to kill.

BOTH CAMPS

The heron:
One foot on land one
In the museum
Of the sea.

HALF MEASURES

Above high-tide mark on the long beach
There is one old shoe.
Someone of little faith
Has gone for a long walk on water.

RECIPROCAL ACTIONS

From midnight on –
Trying to pick the stony lock of sleep...

The clouds and the stars:
Pillowed on the slumbering sea.

COLD WINTER NIGHT

We cannot see them
But even behind the mountain
The moon has friends.

POEM FOR FRED WHITEHEAD

I travelled a long time
In an empty land –

Then, finally –
What a mountain!

THE LONGING

Where is my grasshopper's song?
I look out:
Flowers all down...

Snow!

WINTER GOODNIGHT

The first deep frost
Of a cold autumn
Beautiful! On the flowers and grass.

But I miss the last song
Of my frozen cricket...

MOVING THE IMMOVABLE

A sudden shudder
In the fur of the far ridge –
Oh yes...
The deer are travelling!

THE PROTECTION OF SOFT
AND SIMPLE THINGS

The leaves are falling.
I hear the trains:
Coming closer to the house...

When the last leaf comes down –
Look out!
They'll be in the yard –
In the living room!

GOOD NEWS FROM HELL!

Central
Heating!

ANOTHER REVELATION

In the woods:
Windless cold,
The snow brittle
Under my feet.

Then a little pile of scat —
Steaming!

ON THE ICE FLOE

He was following a great white bear –
Or dreamed it.

And now he is drifting on the cold vast deep
Into the unknown sea.

TRANSFORMATIONS

On the familiar walls,
The tired old graffiti.

Mysterious. . .
Untranslatable –
After the sleet storm.

60 BELOW

So cold tonight –
The sounds of bells
Fall like shot birds.

DOWN RIVER

Worn-out canoes
Empty life jackets.
Last flower petals.
And first dead leaves.

Drifting down...
Below the rapids...

EATING ALONE

No father mother
brothers sisters –
no watermelon!
no whiskey soda

A TRIBUTE

Dunno about those other birds
But you sure scared hell out of me
You punkin head bastard!

MAYBE

The empty field in the snow. . .
A kind of cry. . .
Must be the scarecrow.

STYLE

What do you mean –
Standing around there in those raggedy-ass clothes
Scarecrow?

IT'S A HARD WORLD

Do you have an alibi
For the time the victim was

      Conceived?
      Gestated?
      Born?
      Named?

Claimed as your child?

O OZYMANDIUS!

That huge new billboard
Framed by
The bend of the river –
Then the blizzard. . .

How pitiful all human works!

HOW TO: I

As we follow,
On the track
Of the beast
With double back

Of the beast
Without a front—
What would you expect:
If you keep count?

WHAT HAPPENED TO THE OTHER TWO COMRADES?

Toward Easter now...
The last of the first snow
Crucified in the fields
Already turning black...

OLD ENEMIES

The water may be in love with fire –
But not
With the last of the winter ice.

WAITING

In November
Something
In the empty house
Opens the doors...
To the night wind,
To the moonlight,
To what no one remembers any more...

THE MAN IN THE BLIZZARD

Even his tracks are gone!
And, of course, his shadow...
But he keeps walking around,
Searching
Certain that someone
(Himself perhaps)
Was here before –
Or will be.

GENERATIONS

Spring: in the late wet snow
A confident slip of narcissus...
Nesting... in the dead ruined columns
Of last year's vegetable
Glory

ADVICE FOR THOSE
FACING THE COMING FLOOD

Swimming won't help.
Drown.

Or learn to walk on water.

FLYING HOME

It wasn't you, Lionel Hampton, who taught me to fly!
– But here I am, heading west, over the Atlantic
Trying to catch up with the moon.

I will have the motion of this airplane always in my body,
As I fall down this long chute always toward that fabled and
        vanishing time.

GOING WITH THE FLOW

Only a part of the
Whole
Coil
Is required when the rope
Hangs
The one they've agreed to call
Outlaw.

POWER

for Alvaro in New Mexico

Just a few words!
A world rises . . .
And another falls.

THE GHOST

He comes here
often.
Reluctantly.
With much pain from the cold.
Remembering a place
where
Once
There was a small but perfect
fire.

I NOTICED SOMEWHERE BEFORE

When the leaves fall,
We see the bodies
Of those who were hanged.
But only then.

AMONG THE REASONS FOR BEING

That's what we are:
Seeds in the cold wind...

    The wind always blowing...

BUTTERFLY OR EMPEROR?

After he leaped off the cliff
He was a long time wondering:
Was he falling when he thought he was flying?
Or flying when he thought he was falling?

DEAR WILLY

The Emperor's misers close their murder shops.
In bloody moonlight workers forge a bird
To set upon a barbwire fence to crow
Of what's long gone, or going; or to go.

EVIDENCE

Where Rome was burning...
This tiny exhausted star...
Fallen into the ground.

MORE EVIDENCE

A bruise
On the winter-evening sky...
A crow
Crossed here
About noon.

DESTINY

Those great European trees—
For centuries (unknown to shipbuilders or geographers)
They kept in their secret hearts
The names of the unknown continents!

WARNING

So –
You recognize my footprint . . .
But don't think that you know
Which way I've gone!

POEM

I hear a heavy knocking
In the midnight river.
Something I've never known
Is coming home.

REVOLUTIONARY ACTION

Singing its own song,
The anvil dances
When the hammer has fallen asleep.

THE GOOD OLD DAYS

have always been here:
(moon perfect the sun always
those apparently cuddly squirrels
& the trees without diseases)
each with a knife in its pocket.

REVISIONIST POEM

                              —POPE

The proper study
Of mankind
Is

Women
. . . and men.

INHERITANCES

Among the poor
Many wear second-hand shoes.
Among the very poor
The shoes wear second-hand feet.

A LITTLE KNOWLEDGE

High on his watershelf
The fish shudders.
In the book of sleep,
He is reading a chapter on deserts.

SONG OF THE OPEN ROAD

—for Reg Gibbons

Protected from all running dogs
Through Hell and through Gone I go:
Guided by the great Saint Yes
And his master: great Saint No.

III

NIGHT MEETING

Through different streets that are all alike we walk down toward
        the docks:
Past the drunks sleeping on the subway gratings, past
The hookers like plastic flowers burnt out by the neon of bars:
Streets that are streaked with cold rain, ice, the filthy snow of cities,
Or steaming in the abyss of dead summer heat dog days stinking
        August:

By separate streets we descend through this pain and torment:
Past the blocks of burnt-out cars without wheels or
        motors – childrens' playgrounds,
Down past the gutted tenements where the darkness gapes
On open ground-floors clotted with rubble. Furtive movements of
        rats
Junkies drunks punks broken down whores, poor peoples pushers
        their night medicine cops pay-offs casual murder
These night-black colonies lined with garbage spiced by excrement
These homes for the homeless where they sleep in peril
Men women and children starving shivering sweating pillowed by
        stone
Their sleep troubled by rats rape knives by screams
Like sheets ripped from a tin roof by a cyclone cries of hunger sex
        despair,
The laments of millions encaged in false consciousness
In cells of priestly fraud and patriotic prisons
All the grand night music of the dying culture of money

So we descend on different streets through the guts of the great
        misery machine,
The spontaneous sweat-combustion engine of capitalism,
Where the neon tells us, and the poet, in sorrow, irony and anger:

"We are the greatest city, the greatest nation, nothing like us ever
     was!"
All of which must be changed.

So we descend, till, almost at the bottom, just up from sea level,
We enter the house of an unemployed carpenter
Across from the old waterfront longshoremen's bar *The White
     Horse.*
One by one we enter sit and wait
Until the last one of us comes in sweating, dripping or freezing
And the organizer says "OK, comrades; the group is complete. Time
     to begin."

WORKING IN DARKNESS

I think of the ones like the poet John Haines,
During those long years in Alaska,
Working alone in a cold place,
Sitting in darkness outside the pool of light:
Ice-Fisherman facing the empty hole of the page,
Patient, the spear poised, waiting for a sign.

And coal miners go out in the cold darkness
In search of fire and light.
In darkness they return to their homes.
The long years go by in the night that is under the earth
But they remember the sun.

And I think of my grandfather – how we planted potatoes
By the dark of the moon: each silvery wedge with an eye
To see on their journey and guide them quick to the sun,
As when, building the great ships, I hunted the signs
To weld the galvo or rivet the plates to the deck.

A kind of searching, translation of signs, a kind of hunting:
As when the bowman peers through the night-bound forest:
Reading the sounds of a shaken bush or a rattle of stones,
Patient and impatient driven and hungering, following
Through the cold day and the moon-patched colder night,
The wounded beast his calling says pursue
Though he have nothing to eat in the hunt but its bloody droppings.

LONGING

In these days,
When the winds wear no wedding rings,
Everything seems to be going away:
My sweet son filling his sails at a distant college,
My springtime friends on trail to the ultimate West,
And, even in central summer,
I feel the days shortening,
The stealthy lengthening of the night.

And so, in the imperial extension of the dark,
Against which, all my life, I opposed my body,
I long to pass from this anguish of passings
Into the calm of an indifferent joy...

To enter October's frail canoe and drift down
Down with the bright leaves among the raucous wildfowl
On the narrowing autumn rivers where, in these longer nights,
Secretly, in the shallows or on reedy shorelines,
Ice is already forming.

LATE ARRIVAL

Christ what a distance to have come to arrive at this
                              Godforsaken place!
Forty years on the plains and in the
                    mountains – A wall-to-wall nothing –
And arrive here with what?
This miserable cargo of
                    empty wells!

THE CHILDREN OF CONTEMPORARY CITIES

Grow up not knowing what time of year it is –
Unless it is winter.
That perishing dingy green they sometimes see
May be "grass" (though *that* they recognize)
Or displaced seaweed from some old horror movie.

All the animals are in the zoo and none from this continent,
Unless there is the odd buffalo.
Later they learn about horses from the Mounted Police.
The birds are sparrows
                        except for the pigeons
                                                where
Are the crows?
"The soul suffers when deprived of nature," the philosopher says.

Familiars of rats and cockroaches these
Children would be in wordless terror or crickets.
("Boy Tormented By a Nightingale" – the painter knew.)
For them a tree is only Something upright and changing –
Mysteriously related to snow but having no family name.

But some *do* know.
Out in the city parks with the larch, the hemlock and willow,
Kindling to each tack of weather and turn of the season,
Gravely awake to seed time and harvest,
Aware of the resurrection of grass and the fall of a leaf,
Alive to nature: the muggers and rapists wait.

RECALL

I remember that summer
When you built a backyard teepee
From wind-fall branches and Morning Glories.

Since then, of course,
Everybody has moved
On.

But the Morning Glories
Still raise their tent...
A little more ragged each year.

THAT WEEK IN THE DESERT

Loving in the morning;
Loving at night.
At noon:
Sleeping
Flower-watching
or FOOD!

The afternoons pass
Slow as an English novel.
At midnight,
Sweat cooling,
We walk
Under the moon

Or stars. . .
Or:
At least
Clouds:
Or darkness.

I suppose this might have been. . .
Love.
But what did we know
About that?

USELESS PASSIONS

At sunrise
The shadows
That slept all night in the deep woods
Run away from home.

All morning the trees
Lean away to the west.
The shadows, in the shadowless noon –
Little invisible birds in the branches –
Rest for a moment.

Then they begin the long trek to the east.
Toward evening, growing heavy,
They create the eastern mountains.

Already they are dreaming of leaves:
The first syllables of the night.

ANOTHER CHRISTMAS CAROL

And christmas continues its atrocities...

Now comes a flood of black-clad singers: the ladies so pale and plain we despair of the landscapes that made them, and the gents looking every inch a gelded deacon. Holding their books as if to break them over the heads of their cohorts, they attack the text.

Since they have been singing a prose text, the music has comfortably fallen to the prosaic level and plods along without raising its (or anyone's) eyebrows. But now the music has come to a place where it can canter into an allegro or even a kind of gallop, and since the text has the word "sheep" in it, visions of lambikins must have danced in the composer's head.

The conductor, a kind of prancing twinkletoes in black bondage, who conducts more with his feet than his hands, gives a little leap into the air, his hair swishing like a spooked horse. The eyes of the choir roll up, their backs arch, and every time the word "sheep" appears in the text (and it is the only *substantial* word in the text) this posse comes on in full cry: like mad sheep-punchers in pursuit of this savage maverick outlaw *sheep.*

And so it goes: the sopranos in their sheep-shearer's hysterias, the deep grumbling of the butcher bassos, the mysterious plotting of the contraltos, the little psychotic yelpings of the tenors...

At last they are in agreement: the lamb is sheared and shorn, soothed and seethed in its blood, marinated (with a bit of bay leaf and thyme) and diced up for a shish-kabob or your basic backyard bar-b-q.

Rejoice! Rejoice! Rejoice!

We are washed in the blood of the lamb!

BIRTHDAYS

I see you there,
Little one,
Shy but not lonely,
Hidden – half-hidden – in the folds of your mother's dress.

So many like you...
Waiting in the shadowy reeds...
Like Moses:
Basket cases,
Afraid to begin the long journey toward the king's daughter.

How long will you wait –
Protected in the mothering darkness –
While your father,
Out in the bitter sun,
Dances in lust and rage drunk with love for you –
Awaiting your coming forth?

A PROMISE

All my life — noisy!
Walking around the world in my heavy shoes!
Now I grow lighter,
And I begin to see
How, in that farther sunlight,
I shall move faster and faster
Until my shadow runs on alone
Without even an echo.

GRAVEYARD SHIFT

After working a long time at my desk near the window
I turn out the lamp

slowly
reluctantly
but eventually
the dark sky and the page I have been working on
are flooded
with light!

     *   *   *

Let us turn over the page
And see what is written
On the other side of the night.

FAITHFULLY YOURS

I don't know how's by you but it seems to me
A long time I've been waiting here for the promised Space Lift –
That glorious transport – O'er prison walls I would fly –
Beyond the shadow of flags to distant and different stars.

I haven't been titivating by that mountain pool nor ever
Been found genuflecting to my image in that sweet and sacred water.
The sound of gunfire unsilvers all mirrors. The pain of others
Is mirror enough. And the waiting. Solitude. Lonesome times.

It's a lonesome old world as the old song says: waiting for transport.
But time and again a friend brightens a dark door:
Someone from back then or here now or never before
Enters and the heart of the heartless world stops in that instant.

Comrade, way-faring stranger, fellow traveller, compañero I'm glad
To see you and if I were Japanese I would bow and make tea.
But I'm not and don't have none and so we must take potluck.
Nothing bad about that. We've shared the same fire so long.

So the night moves and the stars grind in their courses.
We keep the home fires burning here in the vast republic
Of the wretched of the earth. We talk till the sky reddens with
        morning.
Impassioned talk. And the changeless stars may be changed. A little.

IN THE CONFUSION OF EMPIRES

Forts become castles
Castles forts...

It goes on:
Crenulation
Fenestration
Even ventilation.

Styles change:
Redesigned by
Gunpowder:
By greed by suffering by
Struggle...
Rise and fall...
Empires
Breasts
Yoni and lingam
Wither...

The wave builds
Fails
Falls away...

And all the while,
Men, in different costumes,
On opposite sides of the river
Feed the war horses
Of the Great King
Of the Great Khan.

LOOK ON MY WORKS!

1.

Once I was like a revolutionary party:
The delegates assemble, vote, the Line is worked out;
Then: forward!
Head and Heart have agreed: Ready!
Ready! say Imagination and Spirit.
Ready, Comrades Hands? *Ready!*
Ready! says the Comrade Body. *Let's Go!*

2.

Now all's in dispute – I'm like a declining empire
Falling apart in its last days. Rebellion
In the backlands, discipline faltering at the frontiers,
The language changing and the passwords lost.
The chain of command broken the very heartland,
An uneasy confederation, breaking up...
– The Goingunder of the western lands!...
Sundown, out there in the far deserts...

*   *   *

The imagination, trapped in a burning building, cries out...
Consciousness, furtive as the dark, invades the City,
Peers out from fallen temples, from the splendid ruins.

NOTES ON THE REVOLUTION

1.

The people want to shoot;
But the bourgeois will not
Climb into the muzzle of the rifle.

2.

The rope of the cowpuncher
Has fallen in love.
With a different kind of neck.

3.

Long trains full of coffins.
Waiting. On sidings...
Covered with weeds.

A MOMENTARY LOSS OF BELIEF IN THE WISDOM OF THE COMMON PEOPLE AND A CURSE ON THE BASTARDS WHO OWN AND OPERATE THEM

"War is the continuation of policy by other means."
So said Von Clausewitz.

But war is also
The continuation of false consciousness
And falsified policy and politics
And greed masked as bourgeois generosity
By the falsified desires of American imperialism
By presidents wedded to cowboys and missiles
By chauvinist beer salesmen peddling the stars and stripes by
   the six-pack
By the trained psychopathic liars of the State Department
By simple-minded sods in all fifty states
By the born-simple clergy and suckers of religion
By the bearded dons and Ph.D. dumdums of Academia
By painters selling third-hand Da Da at fancy prices
By poets who have forgot their songs in their gilded cages
By farmers sold out and put on the road and still finding their enemy
   in Nicaragua or El Salvador
By workers given their walking papers for life and their heads still so
   unscrewed they think the enemy is Russia or Communism
By housewives pissing their pants and dreaming of Red Terror
Or hijackers invading Podunk

By other means.
Politics is the continuation of war by other means.

And now, you celebrated American jackasses:
You still want war?
Go let a hole in the head shed light on your darkling brain –
Remember Vietnam?

Go and be damned!
But don't count on me for nothing you righteous
       stupid sons of bitches!

Inside the white marble ring of a Pope, there is, as there
has always been, a tiny stairway leading down. . .

One kiss and the lid of the ring pops up – even, or perhaps
most likely, the lid of the ring of the First Pope of the CIA,
our present pontiff, the latest version of all those anti-Polish
jokes.

And so the steps lead down, toward secret water. And each
step the nominative, dative, genitive, accusitive, ablative,
and then those faint-away classic Latin verbs: *descendere,*
dare, dare, dare: ending in black water – but, careful!

Ah, here is a great septuagenitalial Greek porch swept free
of all Stoics, a plaza, bonebright, prechristian, where the
spectral mustangs of the noncommittal moon are browsing
on the shadow-grass that grows as an echo of their manes. . .

But the steps continue down, on black and barbarian
stone – a steeper pitch since the Pope's hand grows heavier
as we move down, down, down toward the sunless sea.

A few encampments here. Smell of dung. Turf-fires. One
plank walks out on the dark lagoon where butterfly nets of
fishermen catch (always) the single star and a few fish – or
shrimp stunting in the smoky light.

You may hear the singing – if you come this way, if you
descend the infernal stairs to the dreamy villages of the
poor; or if you go farther: to the port, the great ships to the
other countries and continents of the dispossessed. . . There
is nothing else here, inside the papal ring.

But you will notice – if you notice such things – that none
of the singing is in Latin, and that, along with the *We Shall*
Overcomes and the *No Pasarans,* a vast cursing against
priests and landlords rises: to strike the stony heavens inside
the papal ring.

PROBABLE CAUSE

In the house of the man with no hands
Why are there so many filthy
Dishes:
Tea cups coffee cups wine
glasses plates left over
pieces of stale bread?

Because so many loving
and delightfully thoughtless people
Come to visit here.

A SULLEN MUSIK

Hammers in the morning.
Flutes in the afternoon –
But only on holidays.
Too much of being alive
Stolen away by life;
Too much of life by the job –
Too much of the job
By the hammers of morning.

MORE PAYCUTS AND UNEMPLOYMENT

The Norwegian nightingale
Which Garrison Keillor
Heard singing:
"I t'ink so.
I t'ink so...probably..."
Now sings:
"I now know fuckin well!"
Singing among the elders and the starving masses near
        Lake Wobegon.

FOR A DANCER

Terrifying abandonments
Of flesh to spirit...
In those great leaps
You seem almost
To leave your body!

I would like to be the air around you
That helps you soar...
Now I know it is not the wing
That lifts the bird into flight!

READING BY MECHANIC LIGHT

In the early evening
The dark comes in like a heavy tide...
The blackness empty of god –
Thank god – that dismal bed
We used to smother in.

And now the full moon
Godless – no witches' moon –
Pitches over the houses like an empty ship:
Darkening the stars in the heavens' empty
Spider web.

The moon like a white bone...
Now not even a witch –
Ditched into darkness, bald as a skull.
How does it pull from pole to pole,
The careless sea?

But it has the sea in thrall:
Leashed like a small dog.
And so the tides must thole
In durance vile – as we
Endure our bankruptcy –

Now neither goddess or witch –
And precious little light
To read on a page of stars
What once we dreamed was ours:
Before the light went out.

GOING TO BED IN THE DARK

Laughing: "Not fair!"
The little boy says,
As he climbs on his father's
Kiss to his bed.
"Not fair!" though all night
He will play his plays
In the dream fields
Of his dreaming head.

His father agrees;
It is *not* fair
That one day *he*
Will be forced away,
To climb through the dark
Up a dark stairs
Past all the joys
That echo there

And come at last
Unto that place
Where nothing remains
Of those joyful days.
And father and son
Are grown face to face:
Prisoners of sad
Mortality.